CRONYISM IS a relatively new issue for the conservative movement. While long worried about burdensome regulations and taxes, the right has only recently grown concerned about the improper networks connecting the government and special interests. Of course, conservatives have opposed cronyism in specific instances over the decades. For instance, they complained about farm subsidies as early as the 1950s, and they celebrated the 1986 Tax Reform Act because it eliminated tax breaks for many special interests. Still, thinking about cronyism as a general issue is of recent vintage.

The first conservative critiques of cronyism began around 2006. In *The K Street Gang,* Matt Continetti attacked the relationship between congressional Republicans and lobbyists, and in *The Big Ripoff,* Timothy P. Carney detailed how the government favors special interests. Combined, they signaled growing conservative frustration that the "Republican revolution" had facilitated bigger government and

more corruption. The Troubled Asset Relief Program of 2008 exacerbated these worries. While many believed this program to be necessary, conservatives of all stripes thought it a bitter pill to swallow. Government favoritism toward the housing and financial-services industries had precipitated an economic collapse, and here was Uncle Sam bailing out its own cronies.

Then came the Barack Obama administration. For the two years that Obama, Nancy Pelosi, and Harry Reid ran the government, it was as if Tammany Hall had descended upon the Potomac River. Suddenly, cronyism was everywhere. From the stimulus to Obamacare to Dodd-Frank to the IRS scandal, it seemed as if Obama's cronies had taken complete control over public policy. That is when cronyism emerged as a major issue on the right, generating an explosion of serious work. Carney, Peter Schweizer, Michelle Malkin, and David Freddoso all wrote accounts detailing the pernicious links between the government and special interests. The *Washington*

Examiner and the *Washington Free Beacon* started tracking down bad actors on a daily basis. The Tea Party waves of 2010 and 2014 produced senators like Mike Lee and Tom Cotton, who made cronyism a centerpiece of their political campaigns.

This hardly marks the start of the fight against cronyism. Ralph Nader and his allies have been railing against "corporate welfare" for a half century. Before him, Teddy Roosevelt's Progressive Party bemoaned the "invisible government" of "corrupt interests ... owing no allegiance and acknowledging no responsibility to the people." Nearly a century before T. R., Andrew Jackson had denounced the capacity of government "to grant titles, gratuities, and exclusive privileges, to make the rich richer and the potent more powerful." Before Old Hickory, Thomas Jefferson and James Madison had been deeply worried about corruption in the Bank of the United States.

In other words, cronyism is an old issue, even if conservatives are relatively new to it. As a public-policy problem, it should not be

Cronyism is an old issue, even if conservatives are relatively new to it. As a public-policy problem, it should not be taken lightly.

taken lightly. Jefferson, Madison, Jackson, and Roosevelt all fought cronyism, yet it still vexes the body politic. So if we hope to deal with it, we need to understand it better.

* * *

A sensible starting point is Aristotle. In *The Politics,* he categorizes a *polis* (civic body) by answering two questions: First, is the sovereign a single person, a few elite, or the people at large? Second, on whose behalf does this sovereign rule?

> *On this basis we may say that when the One, or the Few, or the Many rule with a view to the common interest, the constitutions under which they*

do so must necessarily be right constitutions. On the other hand the constitutions directed to the personal interest of the One, or the Few, or the Masses, must necessarily be perversions.

By this reckoning, cronyism is a perversion of good government. *Merriam-Webster* defines *cronyism* as "the unfair practice by a powerful person (such as a politician) of giving jobs and other favors to friends." When politicians use their authority to benefit their associates rather than the people at large, that is cronyism. Because you usually have to have money to make friends with politicians, cronyism is typically a type of oligarchy, which Aristotle defines as the rule of the wealthy.

The question of what to do about cronyism has long troubled political philosophers. The framers of our Constitution did not use the word *cronyism*, but they understood how government could be perverted in such ways. Madison in particular was worried about factions distorting policy for their own ends. Factionalism, he argues in *Federalist* No. 10, is "sown into the nature of man," which means that the promotion of public virtue is only of limited efficacy. The best way to deal with this problem is a "well-constructed Union," which may "break and control the violence of faction." In other words, all people are self-interested and will try to pervert government toward their interests; what we need, therefore, are rules that keep this from happening.

Prior to Madison's age, cronyism had been a common problem in monarchies. The king's favorites often established a court faction that could rule against the common good. England's Glorious Revolution strongly cut down on the sovereignty of the king, but new problems soon emerged, thanks to the development of international trade and the market economy. This was a boon for Europe, and many governments adopted a mercantilistic model to direct the economy. Britain, for instance, kept tight control over her American colonies with the Navigation Acts and directed the flow of trade via royally chartered organizations like the East India Company, which was enormously profitable for

Britain and created many a fortune for those who invested in it. This in turn gave it enormous political power, as these wealthy nabobs entered the House of Commons with an eye to protecting the company.

This mixing of public and private interests led to cronyism. By the 1760s the company was struggling, so the nabobs lobbied for a bailout, which the government supplied. The Tea Act of 1773 allowed the company to dump its surplus directly into North America, rather than through secondary merchants. Moreover, the Tea Act retained the Townshend duties on tea sold in the colonies. Lord North, the British Prime Minister, thought he had killed two birds with one stone: the company could unload its surplus, and the American colonists would implicitly accept Parliament's right to tax them (as the company's tea would still be cheaper than that of its competitors, even with the tax). Yet North had gravely miscalculated. Boston merchants and the Sons of Liberty sneaked into Boston Harbor in December 1773 and dumped more than 300 crates of tea into the water. This event, later named the Boston Tea Party, would be a milestone in America's path to independence. It was also one of the nation's first experiences with cronyism.

As an independent nation, the United States would similarly bestow government charters upon corporations, and cronyism was a predictable result. In 1790, Treasury Secretary Alexander Hamilton proposed the Bank of the United States, an ingenious institution that would secure the nation's perilous finances by linking the financial and commercial elite to the new government. Yet it was a breeding ground for cronyism, as those with insider knowledge of the bank's activities enriched themselves. Jefferson and Madison were outraged and hotly opposed the bank during the 1790s, but the demands of modernization were too pressing for them to dismantle it. As president, Jefferson kept the bank in place, and Madison even chartered the Second Bank in 1816. This, too, was prone to cronyism, as bank managers rewarded their political friends at the expense of the nation's financial well-being. Meanwhile, state governments chartered corporations left and right – not only banks, but also new companies to build canals, bridges, and railroads. Insiders made vast fortunes on their political connections, making state-based cronyism even more pernicious than the federal variety.

The problem was that the government's new economic ventures typically supported public ends through private means. In such undertakings, the distinction between the two often becomes blurry. Those who make a private fortune from a public undertaking are compelled to invest a portion of their subsidies into the political process to protect their benefits. For instance, the First Bank secured the nation's finances via the Northeastern elite, who used their profits to influence the government. Jefferson warned George Washington that Hamilton's Treasury was distributing bank shares to create "an influence of his department over the members of the legislature" in order to keep the bank's charter from being altered or revoked. Meanwhile, Madison predicted, "the stock-jobbers will become the pretorian band of the Government, at once its tool and its tyrant; bribed by its largesses, and overawing it by clamours and combinations."

Jefferson and Madison were striking at an essential aspect of modern cronyism. It is a *conflict of interest*, which directly relates to the scope of the government's purpose. In his veto message for the Second Bank, Jackson praised a government that would "confine itself to equal protection, and, as Heaven does its rains, shower its favors alike on the high and the low, the rich and the poor." Such a night-watchman state would likely not fall prey to cronyism, but it also would not do many tasks we take for granted, including developing the economy. When the government does that – by chartering corporations, imposing protective tariffs, subsidizing exports, or whatever – it inevitably distributes benefits unequally. These may be public-spirited measures to grow the economy, but they use some faction for that purpose. In theory, everybody benefits at least a little bit from such initiatives, but those whom the government directly employs benefit more. They are naturally prone to become cronies

---

The Boston Tea Party would be a milestone in America's path to independence. It was also one of the nation's first experiences with cronyism.

---

to protect their subsidy.

Another lesson from the early republic is that mass-based democracy facilitates cronyism. If government activism creates a supply of cronies, democracy creates a demand for them among politicians. The modern campaign poses enormous logistical and financial challenges to office seekers, in an example of what economists call the collective-action dilemma. The money and manpower required to win an elective office are simply staggering, and have been for a long time. This problem became particularly acute in the 1820s, when the presidency became fully democratized. Jackson generated the effort needed to wage his successful campaign by developing the spoils system, which distributed government jobs to campaign loyalists. Faced with a raucously democratic electoral process, politicians from all across the country embraced Jackson's program. Pretty soon, all manner of jobs and contracts were distributed based on how much somebody had helped the campaign. After the Civil War, patronage birthed massive statewide political machines, where party bosses ruled with an iron fist.

This was cronyism on a massive, *systemic* level, the likes of which the world had never seen before. The effect on public administration was enormously detrimental. For starters, the heavy turnover at government agencies meant that the workload had to be left to a clique of low-level, permanent staffers. In addition to that, the party expected a lot in return from its workers. They had to kick a portion of their salary back to the party and set their public duties aside during campaign season. And then there was the graft. To appreciate the scale of embezzlement during this period, consider the New York Customs House, which collected much of the nation's tax revenues. By subjecting public administration to partisan politics, the spoils system legitimized fraud at the customs house on a massive scale. Customs agents would intentionally undervalue imports, then make "official" discoveries of the error. They received a cut of the bounty, with the expectation that they kick some back to the party. The customs house kept Republican boss Roscoe Conkling atop New York politics for 15 years, and it made all the top party brass rich.

And then, in an instant, the whole thing fell apart. The spoils system had been a cause of outrage from the moment it started, but nobody had been able to stop it. The Whigs complained about Jackson in the 1830s, the Republicans complained about James Buchanan in the 1850s, the Liberal Republicans complained about Ulysses S. Grant in the 1870s. But the regime endured – until a crazy person assassinated President James Garfield in 1881. The assassin claimed to have been a member of the pro-patronage faction of the Republican Party, though in truth he was simply insane. Public outrage boiled over, and Congress passed the Pendleton Civil Service Reform Act, which eventually eliminated most federal patronage jobs. States followed suit, and by the middle of the 20th century, the bureaucracy was mostly professionalized and insulated from politics.

While Pendleton was a victory for good government, the success was short-lived. It remained a stark reality that politicians had to fund their campaigns, and the need for campaign cash only increased as the population grew and new communication technologies proliferated. Without access to patronage, politicians began aggressively courting those looking to profit from the government's economic activism. Today, millions of dollars are required to saturate television with campaign messages, finely tuned by professional consultants who charge top dollar. For such expansive financing, politicians inevitably rely heavily on interest groups.

Meanwhile, the Industrial Revolution made business more dependent upon government. Businesses became vast conglomerates that spanned the nation, which meant they inevitably fell under the Interstate Commerce Clause. They also needed favorable tax rates, beneficial monetary policy, and heavy infrastructure investment. Thus, they developed powerful lobbying operations to pressure the federal government. These outfits were informal at first, usually depending upon personal relations between executives and politicians, but over the past 80 years, these networks have been largely supplanted by sophisticated, highly specialized lobbying organizations that acquire as much from the government as possible.

Moreover, the scope of federal authority began to increase. Hamilton's proposal for the national government to develop the domestic economy was controversial in the 1790s, but a century later it was widely accepted. The progressive movement substantially broadened the government's regulatory power, and the New Deal expanded this authority even more. The government also began dispensing social-welfare benefits via minimum-wage guarantees, union protections, Social Security, and the like. As federal power grew, more groups faced the same incentives as businesses: their well-being depended directly upon the policymakers in Washington, so they had to become "friends" with politicians.

These factors – expensive campaigns without patronage, the rise of big business, and the expansion of government power – generated the current variant of cronyism. Modern cronyism combines the oligarchy of mercantilism with the spoils system's subjugation of public administration to electoral politics. Desperate to secure their well-being and re-election, today's politicians sell public policy to the highest bidders. This institutionalized

Desperate to secure their well-being and re-election, today's politicians sell public policy to the highest bidders.

conflict of interest touches almost every policy domain: taxes, regulation, infrastructure grants, science and technology spending, support for businesses, farm subsidies, social-welfare programs, and even military appropriations. There are hundreds of special interests, employing thousands of lobbyists, constantly clamoring for favors from the government. And Uncle Sam happily obliges. To borrow that line from Madison, modern interest groups are the new "pretorian band of the Government, at once its tool and its tyrant; bribed by its largesses, and overawing it by clamours and combinations."

Far from being illegal, this practice is widely accepted, with the informal norm being that the benefits politicians reap from special interests must be removed by several degrees from themselves. For instance, politicians cannot accept personal checks from interest groups, but groups may donate to their campaigns, which indirectly benefit politicians and are sometimes even run by their families and friends. Politicians may not accept gratuities beyond a very small amount from lobbyists, but after they leave office, they can collect multimillion-dollar paydays by working for lobbyists. Politicians cannot knowingly profit from government appropriations or regulations, but in practice such violations are common, because only the most egregious are provable.

Congress is the locus of cronyism, with the committee system being a particular problem. Congressional committees have substantial power over their policy domains. Their members have more knowledge than the average legislator, so they provide important cues on how to vote. Committees also determine the specifics of policy: while amendments on the floor of the House and Senate can alter committee products, committees usually have the final say over the details. What's more, committee leaders typically helm the conference committees that the two chambers use to finalize legislation. This combination of specialization and authority generally helps Congress do its business, but it facilitates cronyism in two ways. First, it enables interest groups to concentrate their lobbying efforts and campaign cash. Thus, banks focus on the Financial Services Committee and ignore the Agriculture Committee, while agribusinesses do the opposite. Second, it enables "high demanders" in the government to squeeze the most out of policies. A union-backed congressman from eastern Ohio goes to the Energy and Commerce Committee, while a Southern California member with defense-industry cronies joins the Armed Services Committee. All told, the committee system helps interest groups pinpoint their resources and ensures that the politicians they target are eager partners.

Cronyism is a bipartisan phenomenon. Democrats mostly controlled Congress from the 1930s until 1994, and they brought modern cronyism into being. Republicans have usually held Congress since 1994 and have entrenched the practice, often at the expense of their public commitment to limited government. For instance, the farm-subsidy program is one example of cronyism that Republicans successfully reformed in 1996 – only to undo it within a few years. In 2014, they passed the most wasteful farm bill in recent memory.

Meanwhile, Washington journalists are usually establishment liberals who do not believe the government needs to be reformed and who want to encourage public faith in it, so they are disinclined to highlight the issue. Compounding this, cronyism usually happens within fine-grained policies, which require technical knowledge that journalists lack. To top it off, journalists depend upon access to politicians, and writing unflattering exposés of cronyism is not a good strategy for career advancement. Thus the grandees of the media are happy to chalk up cronyism to "the way things work."

* * *

Maybe the powers that be are right. Maybe cronyism is just the price of political business. A philosopher like Plato might have had the luxury of sketching out an ideal Republic, but we must deal with the world as it is and try to make the best of it. Hamilton held such a pragmatic view of cronyism, judging it to be necessary for the proper functioning of government. He once told Jefferson and John Adams in a private conversation that the British king's patronage was essential to good government. It was the means by which the monarch could induce narrow-minded legislators to do what was truly in the national interest. In theory, they should not have needed such inducements, but in practice they did. According to this perspective, cronyism is a necessary evil that an actual republic must accept. Similarly, contemporary commentators like Joe Klein and Thomas Edsall

---

Congress is the locus of cronyism, with the committee system being a particular problem.

---

have suggested that earmarks (a form of congressional pork-barrel spending) are necessary to get big pieces of legislation passed.

Yet pragmatism can be overdone, just like idealism. If it is unwise to judge our government against a model that cannot actually exist, it is equally imprudent to apply no standard whatsoever. For his part, Aristotle occupied a middle ground, acknowledging the practical necessities of governance while retaining normative standards by which to judge them. Importantly, Hamilton was not an apologist for cronyism, per se. His defense was predicated upon its necessity to good government, which implicitly assumes that it has not perverted the ends of the *polis*. Similarly, we can acknowledge that some self-interested transactions are necessary for any republic and ask whether cronyism has transgressed this limit. Has it gone on to endanger the republic itself?

There are three reasons to worry that cronyism has indeed gone too far. First, cronyism costs a lot of money, too much for this age of low economic growth and high budget deficits. A precise figure is difficult to estimate, but some examples illustrate just how substantial the premium for cronyism is. Take Medicare, for starters. It is a delegated welfare program that reimburses providers for their expenses in treating patients. Until the 1980s, the program basically paid providers whatever they deemed reasonable, which is why costs went up so much in the 15 years after the program was passed. Then Congress implemented a cost-control system to pay providers based on an estimate of the value of each procedure. This approach has yielded two problems, both of which relate to cronyism. First, the government pays roughly $40 billion per year for improper claims. Second, the providers themselves basically set their own rates, which is an enormous conflict of interest that inflates the costs of the program and medicine in general.

The government could, in theory, take control of the process, developing its own payment schedules and hiring auditors to recover improper claims. But it does not do that – because the medical-services industry is one of the most powerful lobbyists in the country. It provided about $140 million in campaign contributions in the 2014 cycle – more than those of labor, natural resources, or agricultural businesses. It also spent about

$1 billion in lobbying in 2013–14, second only to the financial-services industry. This points to the extraordinary nature of cronyism: for only $1 billion, the health-services industry can secure tens of billions in government rents. The return on this political investment is hundreds, if not thousands, of times better than what the stock market offers, where annual returns rarely exceed 10 percent.

The cost of cronyism often does not even show up in the federal budget. Corporate tax giveaways cost upwards of $100 billion per year, but they are not considered spending. For instance, in 2014 the Tax Foundation estimated that the corporate tax code contains about $45 billion worth of corporate welfare, which is of dubious economic utility. This is not money that is "spent" in a budgetary sense, but it still provides an enormous benefit to recipients. Relatedly, the government looks the other way as U.S.-based corporations aggressively hide domestic profits overseas. This is why profits booked in the Cayman Islands amount to 1,600 percent of its gross domestic product. The money is not earned there, just hidden from the tax man. This is cronyism by inaction. Under pressure from multinational firms, the government leaves tax shelters alone.

The real costs of Obamacare's cronyism are also off budget. Obama cut deals with all manner of interest groups to secure the passage of the Affordable Care Act. The insurers, the hospitals, the AARP, and drug manufacturers won favorable policies in exchange for their political support of and participation in the new program. At the time the bill was passed, the Congressional Budget Office estimated that the law would cost less than $1 trillion in its first 10 years. That figure, high as it is, was actually a gross underestimate of the true cost. Much of it was pushed off the federal books – in the form of higher premiums, deductibles, and co-payments on the individual marketplace. Moreover, a 2014 study by the American Health Policy Institute found that Obamacare was increasing costs for the largest employers by about $5,000 per employee.

The burdens of cronyism can ripple throughout the economy at large. The average citizen overpays on all manner of products – whether it be a gallon of milk, a pair of jeans, an airline ticket, or even a home – because of cronyism. Farm subsidies alter the economic incentives in the agricultural industry, pushing farmers to grow crops and raise livestock that are subsidized by the federal government and increasing the price of many foods. Similarly, the consumer pays a premium for tariffs that prop up a handful of politically connected industries like textiles. Additionally, the Export-Import Bank supposedly helps domestic exporters by providing loans to overseas borrowers, but these can have perverse downstream effects. Ex-Im does a lot of business on behalf of Boeing, which means it helps foreign airlines in competition with domestic carriers like Delta. Finally, Fannie Mae and Freddie Mac aligned with affordable-housing groups, mortgage brokers, and home builders in the late 1990s and early 2000s to encourage the federal government to reduce underwriting standards. This misguided policy inflated home prices, fueled a housing bubble, and ultimately contributed to the Great Recession of 2008–09.

In general, cronyism creates enormous *waste*. The government misallocates scarce resources for political purposes, while interest groups spend heavily on politics rather than on improving their businesses. We all bear this burden, even if we are unaware of it. It is impossible to estimate precisely just how much this costs, but it easily costs hundreds of billions of dollars per year. Ours is an extremely wealthy country, but it is still hard to wave off such waste – especially in an era of persistently weak economic growth, structural deficits, and income stagnation for the middle class.

Cronyism also limits the political debate. In our pluralistic system of government, participation is open to all. Cronyism corrupts this process by giving disproportionate influence to those with the greatest, most personal stake in policies. The result is a constricted public space for discussing our options. When a policy is in need of reform, the only solutions that may be practically considered are those that the dominant interest groups deem acceptable. In plenty of cases, this is not a problem; after all, interest groups can offer perfectly reasonable solutions in many circumstances. But in other instances, this means common-sense fixes are never even mentioned, let alone considered.

Scholars have long understood that the ability to determine the range of options is a very important power. In *The Semisovereign People*, political scientist E. E. Schattschneider termed this the mobilization of bias. He wrote that "the definition of the alternatives is the supreme instrument of power.... He who determines what politics is about runs the country." Cronyism mobilizes bias on a whole host of issues to ensure that certain options are off the table before debate even begins. It therefore diminishes democratic accountability over public policy.

Consider again the example of Medicare. The program is enormously expensive, and the two parties fight endlessly over its price tag, which is projected to balloon over the next half century. Yet neither party complains about the glaring conflict of interest at the heart of the program, which is highly relevant to the problem of cost containment: medical-service providers basically set their own reimbursement rates. This is what $1 billion buys the medical-services industry – bipartisan silence. Medicare is not the only such example. For instance, the nation has lousy policies dealing with food stamps and agriculture because of cronyism. These two distinctive domains have been joined for 50 years in a massive logroll, whereby rural farmers and the urban poor limit the range of reforms that the country may enact in either area, despite their manifest problems. Similarly, the political influence of the financial-

The average citizen overpays on all manner of products – whether it be a gallon of milk, a pair of jeans, an airline ticket, or even a home – because of cronyism.

services industry ensured that the country did not have a robust debate about the causes and consequences of the Great Recession. Instead, the original version of what became the Dodd-Frank law was likely drafted by a Wall Street law firm. Little wonder that it enshrined "too big to fail" for the largest institutions, which not coincidentally spend lavishly on the political process.

Third, cronyism exacerbates economic, social, and political inequality. This is usually not an issue that troubles conservatives, who accept that a dynamic, market-based economy is going to make some men wealthier than others. In the long run – so this argument goes – everybody is better off. Yet this logic has little bearing on cronyism. Political power is of a fixed and finite quantity, which distinguishes it from economic growth. Thus, the conservative apology for economic inequality has no force when it comes to cronyism. What one group gains in power, another *must* lose. Moreover, the inequality of cronyism often works against the dynamic forces of the marketplace. If a man has made his fortune selling widgets and prevails upon the government to keep others from competing against him, he has actually *destroyed* the market, to create a monopoly for himself. Thus, all the dynamism that would have occurred because of competition among widgetmakers disappears. Widgets do not get any better, cheaper, or more reliable. They stay the same, and in that small way, society stagnates because of cronyism, even though the original innovator prospers greatly.

Granted, cronyism need not produce inequality. For instance, while the spoils system had many faults, it generally was a leveling force in which average citizens could participate. But modern cronyism, which derives in part from the old system of mercantilism, is quite different. To be a politician's crony, you must have something he wants. To be precise about it, you must *bid* for his friendship amid intense competition, which means your final bid will have to be quite high. Lobbying shops do not come cheap, after all. So today's cronyism usually reinforces the wealth, power, and status of those who already possess all three. Political scientists have long noted this problem. In *The Semisovereign People,* Schattschneider claimed that "the flaw in the pluralist heaven is that the heavenly chorus sings with a strong upper-class accent." In *The End of Liberalism,* Theodore Lowi argued that our system of government tends to maintain old "structures of privilege" and create new ones, even when the program's ostensible purpose is to help the poor. Inequality may be tolerable for the sake of economic dynamism, but it is an insufferable consequence of cronyism.

* * *

Cronyism is not only a public-policy problem; it is the *essential* problem. Cronyism infests every corner of our government, so in any policy domain where conservatives have an interest – from health care and taxes to education and energy – cronyism is an impediment to sensible reforms. There is no ignoring it.

To date, conservative reformers have notched victories against the excesses of cronyism, in the hopes that they would lead to later successes. In particular, they have invested enormous energy in trying to eliminate the Export-Import Bank. This is a highly vulnerable institution because its benefits go mostly to Boeing. Ex-Im is an egregious form of corporate welfare that has bred rampant cronyism, and it should be gotten rid of. Yet the problem with this strategy is that it is like going after low-hanging fruit:

after that has been plucked, there is little else to do. Indeed, other forms of cronyism – like conflicts of interest in Medicare, the logrolling that connects food stamps to farm subsidies, or federal housing policy – have survived because politically they are much more powerful than Ex-Im. Such programs benefit a large number of groups, which coordinate a vigorous defense against any threats. The fight against Ex-Im succeeded because it pitted determined reformers against (mostly) just Boeing. But to eliminate Medicare overpayments, reformers would have to defeat a vast, interconnected array of interest groups that annually pour a billion dollars into politics.

It is better to view big government programs not as the underlying disease but rather as its symptoms. If we are looking for a cure, we must dig deeper – beneath the programs, to the politicians who create and sustain them. They are the problem, and as already noted, they come from both parties. It is not enough to simply elect more Republicans to Con-

Cronyism infests every corner of our government, so in any policy domain where conservatives have an interest, cronyism is an impediment to sensible reforms.

gress. The country has been doing that for the past 20 years, to little effect. So we must examine the incentive structures of the political class itself and think about how to induce politicians to reduce cronyism. Our focus should not be the great statesmen, those who readily sacrifice their interests for the sake of the public good. Meanwhile, the worst politicians are beyond hope, and many should be prosecuted by the Department of Justice. So we must ponder the average member of Congress, for he is the critical case.

No doubt he has some selfless impulses, but the average politician cares mostly about himself and wants three things above all else: first, money to fund his campaign; second, information, to ensure that he does not vote against his constituents on important matters; and third, personal income that is commensurate with his social standing. Those are the main reasons he collects cronies. They help him achieve these goals, and he gives them public policy in return. On each item, reformers must find ways to restrict his access to cronies and otherwise supply the goods and services he collects from them.

A century of campaign-finance reform has failed to do this, and for good reason. Reformers are often motivated by the highest ideals, but too often they wrongly think the best strategy is simply to limit a candidate's access to funds. This tactic often runs afoul of the First Amendment, and the Supreme Court regularly guts campaign-finance legislation, leaving behind an incoherent hodgepodge that fails to do any good. Moreover, the restrictions themselves inevitably generate loopholes that favor cronyism. In fact, today's campaign-finance regime is a kind of incumbent-protection cartel. By capping the dollar amount of total contributions at a low level, current law forces candidates to collect money from a wide array of donors. Congressmen can easily make such contacts via their committees, but challengers struggle mightily. This is one reason cronyism has gotten worse over the past half century, despite several major campaign-finance reforms. The solutions have exacerbated the problem.

A better approach would be to create alternative sources of campaign funds, under the assumption that if politicians do not have to develop cronyistic relationships to build their war chests, they are less likely to do so. Why not have a refundable tax credit for small donors, capped at $300 per individual, with a federal matching fund to bolster the political power of average citizens? This would impose only a modest burden on the Treasury, and it could scramble the current campaign-finance calculus altogether. Ideally, it would be great for small donors to provide the bulk of a candidate's funds. Their investment in politics is too small to purchase some special favor, so they are typically motivated by a public interest. Moreover, a tax credit would publicly finance campaigns, based on the preferences of taxpayers. This would be an improvement over the patronage system, which lent itself to fraud because politicians controlled the funds, as well as over the presidential financing system, which collapsed because bureaucratic rules and governmental stinginess could not keep up with the rising cost of the modern campaign.

A key job of interest groups is providing information to members of Congress. Our legislature has the authority to weigh in on just about any public-policy problem one can imagine, but doing so in an intelligent fashion requires expertise that the average member of Congress simply lacks. Unfortunately, the legislature does not provide members with those resources: the staff of Congress was only 21,000 as of 2009, less than it was in 1979. This is simply not enough manpower for a member to get timely and accurate answers to policy questions, so he relies inevitably upon interest groups to fill the gaps. The problem is that such information often favors the interests of the group that provides it. On top of this, Congress does not pay its senior staffers a salary that is commensurate with what they could command in the private market, which gives them an incentive to curry favor with interest groups before they leave the public sector. Accordingly, Congress needs a larger staff, and it should pay them more. Expanding congressional staff does not violate conservative norms about limited government; the legislative branch is the closest to the

---

For all intents and purposes, lasting reform will not come until one of the parties makes cronyism a top issue.

---

people, and adding legislative staffers would not transfer power from the people to an unelected bureaucracy but would help elected members serve their constituents better. Plus, doubling the legislative staff would still leave it at a fraction of the executive branch's staff. The Agriculture Department alone has over 100,000 employees.

Finally, reformers must deal realistically with members' personal finances, taking politicians not as we would like them to be but as they are. While most do not intend to become rich from public service, they want an income commensurate with their social status. Right now, members make $174,000 per year. Considering that they must maintain two homes (one in the expensive Washington, D.C., metro area), this leaves many feeling pinched. The squeeze provides an opportunity for cronies, who can win favors by providing for politicians' personal well-being.

In response, reformers should demand a strict ethos of public service. The place to start is with the revolving door. Social scientists have found that before members leave Congress, they often change their behavior to court prospective employers, like lobbyists. Reformers should therefore impose a lifetime lobbying ban upon former members, with an exemption for public-interest groups like Heritage and Brookings. Moreover, the definition of *lobbyist* must be amended to account for the various loopholes that enable former members to lobby without technically being registered. And while in office, members whose assets rise above a certain threshold should be obligated to place them in a blind trust. This is commonplace for presidents, and the same logic applies as forcefully for members of Congress. Finally, the Federal Election Commission should have more staff and resources to audit political committees to prevent members from siphoning money from their campaigns into their bank accounts. Relatedly, its six-member panel should be reduced to five members, so it can be an effective regulatory agency (with a permanent spot for two Democrats, two

Republicans, and one independent).

These suggestions are meant to be illustrative, not comprehensive. Above all, reformers must think carefully about these pathways of corruption – campaign finance, information, and personal enrichment – to develop innovative ways to alter the incentives that the average member faces. Only then will we get a handle on cronyism.

* * *

These reforms are sensible, but are they salable? After all, going after cronyism is to strike at the foundation of modern politics itself. That may be in the public interest, but politicians like the status quo, which is why they will not reform it. How do we get them to accept change?

This is a very old question. In surveying the disastrous state of public affairs in the 1780s, Madison noted that politicians are motivated by "1. Ambition 2. Personal interest. 3. Public good. Unhappily thc two first arc proved by experience to be most prevalent." But he did not despair; instead, he designed a system whereby the ambitions and personal interests of politicians would promote the public good. He argues in *Federalist* No. 51, "Ambition must be made to counteract ambition," so our system divides power to give politicians competing incentives, thereby "supplying, by opposite and rival interests, the defect of better motives." This is what reformers must now do: adjust the rules of the game so that self-interested politicians actually want to reform the system.

Madison has more to teach. He hoped this system would be self-correcting, but he judged the Federalist Party of the 1790s an existential threat to republican government. He thought it unconstitutionally expanded government authority, passed laws suppressing political opposition, and created a standing army to impose its will on a recalcitrant people. In *The Federalist,* he argues that the recourse against such minorities is the "republican principle" of majority rule. But how to bring that ideal to life? How to rally the people at large to vindicate the public interest? The answer that Madison and Jefferson devised was a *political party.* Their Republican Party (often known by the neologism "Democratic-Republican Party") transformed widespread public dissatisfaction into a forceful political movement.

Opponents of cronyism would do well to heed Madison's counsel. For all intents and purposes, lasting reform will not come until one of the parties makes cronyism a top issue. The parties are the principal way – perhaps the only way – to defend the public interest in the face of rampant factionalism. Conservatives should focus on the Republican Party, whose growing reformist wing led the assault on Ex-Im. Supporting these good-government Republicans would be helpful to the party as a whole. After all, cronyism – as we have noted – tends to favor the wealthy and well connected, whom voters often think of as partial to the Republicans. Standing up to cronyism would help the GOP play against type and maybe win over voters who think the party is too elitist.

Of course, the GOP has been an unreliable supporter of good government over the past 20 years. There are quarters of the party that are interested in reform, but too much of its establishment goes along to get along. What to do about this? Return to Madison's three motives: ambition, personal interest, and the public good. Conservative reformers need to link the ambitions and personal interests of Republican politicians to the public good, and the best way to do that is through *primary elections.* These are powerful yet underused tools to clean house in a party. Lately, reformers have been trying to topple Republican senators who are too comfortable with cronyism, but this may be biting off more than they can chew. The best place to start is with primaries for the House and the state legislatures. These incumbents cannot collect as much money to defend themselves as United States senators can, so it is easier to cashier the lackluster ones. This is not to say that the task would be easy. Conservatives would have to educate themselves about which office-holders are true reformers and which are phonies. They would have to recruit quality challengers, and they would have to commit time and money to securing victory. None of this is easy work, but it is essential in remaking the Republican Party. Total victory would not be required – rather, just enough victories to make those average Republican politicians sensitive to the serious mood of their constituents.

This might strike some conservatives as unappealing. Many are ready to write off the GOP altogether, after 20 years of disappointment. Yet this would be a mistake. We would do well to take our cue from Madison. Reform inevitably requires a political party that is committed to bringing it about, which means that conservatives must work within the Republican Party. This starts with an effort to clean our own house. Then and only then can we clean up the halls of the government, finally striking a blow against the cronyism that has so damaged our republic.

First American edition published in 2015 by Encounter Books, an activity of Encounter for Culture and Education, Inc., a nonprofit, tax exempt corporation.
Encounter Books website address: www.encounterbooks.com

Manufactured in the United States and printed on acid-free paper. The paper used in this publication meets the minimum requirements of ANSI/NISO Z39.48–1992 (R 1997) (*Permanence of Paper*).

FIRST AMERICAN EDITION

LIBRARY OF CONGRESS CATALOGING-IN-PUBLICATION DATA

Cost, Jay.
What's so bad about cronyism? / Jay Cost.
pages cm. — (Encounter broadsides ; 44)
ISBN 978-1-59403-871-6 (pbk. : alk. paper) —
ISBN 978-1-59403-872-3 (ebook)
1. Political corruption—United States. 2. Patronage, Political—United States. 3. Pressure groups—United States. 4. Political culture--United States. I. Title.
JK731.C67 2015
364.1'3230973—dc23
2015028090

10 9 8 7 6 5 4 3 2 1

SERIES DESIGN BY CARL W. SCARBROUGH